T5-AXO-704

A TIME FOR COMMITMENT

In appreciation for your support of
Focus on the Family, please accept this
copy of *A Time for Commitment* by
Ted Engstrom, with Robert C. Larson.
Your contributions enable this
organization to address the needs of
homes through radio, television,
literature and counseling.

On the following pages you will find
practical advice on how to make
positive commitments to God, family and career. We trust this book will
be a valuable addition to your home
library.

Focus on the Family
P.O. Box 500
Arcadia, CA 91006-0500

A Time for Commitment

Ted W. Engstrom

with Robert C. Larson

Zondervan Publishing House
Grand Rapids, Michigan

Daybreak Books are published by
Zondervan Publishing House
1415 Lake Drive S.E.
Grand Rapids, Michigan 49506

A TIME FOR COMMITMENT
Copyright © 1987 by Ted W. Engstrom

All rights reserved. No portion of this publication may be
reproduced, stored in a retrieval system, or transmitted in any
form or by any means—electronic, mechanical, photocopy,
recording, or by any other—except for brief quotations in
printed reviews, without the prior permission of the publisher.

Library of Congress Cataloging in Publication Data

Engstrom, Theodore Wilhelm, 1916–
   A time for commitment.

   Bibliography: p.
   1. Conduct of life. 2. Success. 3. Commitment (Psychology)
I. Larson, Robert C. II. Title.
BJ1581.2.E55   1987   158'.1   86-28165

Cloth: ISBN 0-310-51010-4
Paper: ISBN 0-310-51011-2

Printed in the United States of America

87 88 89 90 91 / EE / 10 9 8 7 6 5 4 3 2

To Dorothy,
who for almost fifty years
has committed herself to God—
and to me

Contents

Contents

Foreword

Commitment is a lost value in American life. Headlines about spy scandals, fragmented families, and corporate fractures are commonplace. Loyalty to family, friends, church, and nation is paid lip-service only—and discarded when it stands in the way of self-fulfillment or self-advancement.

Thus the clear call for Christians today is to stand in radical opposition to this egocentric trend. To be salt and light in today's culture means that our uncompromising commitment to Jesus Christ must show itself in the unity, love, and firm belief that our volatile world so desperately needs.

Ted Engstrom is uniquely qualified to write with conviction and compassion about commitment, for his life is a testimony to that quality. He has been my trusted and faithful friend since my conversion in 1973. As head of World Vision, he displays the fruit of Christian commitment, distributing food and services to needy people around the globe. And in this stimulating book, Ted challenges the Christian church to take a hard look at what such commitment means in everyday life. Taken to heart, such a message can change the character of the Church today—and eventually the nation as well.

Charles W. Colson
Washington, D.C.

Part 1

Discovering *Your* Hidden Key

It is more important to do the
right thing than to do things
right.

Peter Drucker

Introduction

Success, true happiness, and personal fulfillment always leave clues. If anyone has achieved
outstanding success in business, personal relationships, leadership, or other challenges, there
are always good, solid reasons why. Maybe it's the
way that person walks, talks, studies, or listens.
Perhaps it's that special handshake, a confident
stride, a certain sense of purpose, or eye contact
that says, "I see you, hear you, and understand
what you're saying." Whatever the clues may be,
there will always be powerful reasons why someone has met with success.

I want to walk alongside you, my reader-friend,
on a path strewn with hundreds of these extraordinary clues—clues that, I promise, will help
you achieve the success and personal fulfillment
you seek and need.

Surprisingly, some of these clues will be no
further than our fingertips, like diamonds scat-
tered in our own back yards. Other clues will
demand careful detective work. But the keys to
the strongbox of success are all there for us to
discover together.

I believe with all my heart that this small book has the potential to help you change the way you look at yourself and your world. If you're just existing, I'll show you keys to unlock enthusiasm for life. If you're bored, tired, and perhaps cynical, beware! I'll challenge you to a new way of living to help free you from the shackles of those debilitating, destructive attitudes forever. If you've lost your compassion for a world that's sick, hungry, and dying, you'll discover how vitally important *you* are to God's great plan for the salvation and healing of our needy world.

People often ask what drives me to the ends of the earth to serve people who can't even say thank you in English. Let me share President Theodore Roosevelt's words, engraved in my mind and soul for more than forty years.

> It's not the critic who counts; not the man who points out how the strong man stumbled or where the doer of deeds could have done them better. The credit belongs to the man who is actually in the arena; who strives valiantly; who errs and comes short again and again, because there is no effort without error and shortcoming; who does actually try to do the deed; who knows the great enthusiasm, the great devotion, knows in the end the triumph of high achievement, and who, at the worst, if he fails, at least fails while daring greatly. Far better it is to dare mighty things, to win glorious triumphs even though checkered by failure, than to take rank with those poor spirits who neither enjoy much nor suffer much because they live in the gray twilight that knows neither victory nor defeat.

What inspires such character? Beneath this persistent determination and never-say-die attitude lies yet another force—one of the strongest forces we will ever encounter—*commitment.* It's a dynamic commitment to ourselves, our neighbors, and to the world we share. During our search for clues, we'll meet some of the dangers of failing to make positive commitments. We'll experience the thrill of achievement beyond our greatest expectations. And we'll uncover the "evidence of things not seen" placed here by Him who long ago made a spiritual commitment to our physical well-being.

Welcome to the world of commitment.

Commitment in a friendship is surely the most precious treasure of all. Far exceeding the over-rated pleasures of fame and fortune, it stands firm when all else falls to ruin. Such a commitment to each other have Robert C. Larson and I shared for more than fifteen years. Beyond our deep personal relationship, Bob's gift for the written word, as well as his dedication and passion for the material within these pages, has helped place this book in your hands today. To this dear friend, I extend my deepest appreciation.

Join us now as we enter the demanding, rewarding world of commitment . . . your hidden key to personal fulfillment.

T.W.E.

Consider the postage stamp, my son. Its usefulness consists in its ability to stick to one thing until it gets there.

Anonymous

1

Designed for Commitment

While cleaning out her husband's belongings, a widow discovered dozens of keys she couldn't identify. Were they relics from worthless projects long forgotten? Or were they claims to important treasure? How would she ever find out? After exhausting all suggestions, the best she could do was admonish readers of a national newspaper column to take better care of important keys—disposing of worthless ones and marking those of value.

Ironically, our job in this search for the hidden key to personal fulfillment is much the same. Perhaps the key we seek is right there in plain sight. But maybe it's lost on a key ring of convictions that once opened important doors when you "thought as a child."

Edward R. Murrow observed, "The obscure we see eventually. The completely apparent takes longer." Working together, we can speed that process.

What is commitment? Who needs it? And why?

You may have heard the story of the chicken and the pig. The two were walking side by side along a country road when they noticed an announcement tacked on the bulletin board of a little country church. The sign read: Ham and Eggs Breakfast this Sunday at 7:30 A.M. All are invited.

The pig turned to the chicken and said, "Will you look at that! For you, that's no more than a day's work. But for me, it's total commitment."

I can understand the pig's position. Commitment *is* costly, demanding careful focus and discretion. We can't be committed to just anything. Yet recently, we've had a heavy dose of books that focused on how to "Look out for #1" and "How to be our own best friend." But there seems to be an imbalance between those books and the ones that talk about the excitement of being committed to a cause, an idea, or a person. As we continue, we'll see how beneficial, even necessary, it is to improve ourselves to prepare for the greater challenges beyond.

Within ten miles of our World Vision Headquarters in Monrovia, California, stands a living tribute to one man's personal commitment to a greater challenge—the Jackie Robinson Center in Pasadena.

In 1945, the time was long overdue for including Blacks in major league baseball. But the pioneer had to be a rare combination of talent and tact—someone with the athletic ability to speak for itself and the will power to stand back and let it do so.

"It won't be easy," said Branch Rickey of the Brooklyn Dodgers. "You'll be heckled from the bench. They'll call you every name in the book. The pitchers will throw at your head. They'll make it plain they don't like you, and they'll try to make it so tough that you'll give it all up and quit." Then he added sternly, "But you won't fight back either. You'll have to take everything they dish out and never strike back. Do you have the guts to take it?"[1]

Jackie Robinson had the "guts." He courageously endured a storm of abuse for the chance to unlock a new door of opportunity for his race. Venting his hostility through spectacular swings and incredible catches, he became the 1947 National League Rookie of the Year and the 1949 Most Valuable Player, entering baseball's Hall of Fame with a lifetime batting average of .311.[2]

In 1974, the City of Pasadena erected the Jackie Robinson Center in his old neighborhood. Here the first Black in major league baseball continues to provide opportunities for young players even now, more than a decade after his death. All because of commitment.

Promise, submit, permit, mission, remit are cousins to the word "commit." Send or let go in Latin is *mitto* and *missus.* Combined with *co,* (together), commit means to send together. The prefix and root do not work alone; neither do you.

Without the committed care of our parents, we would have quickly perished as newborns. But consider the infant's potential. Although as infants we were unable to feed ourselves, we are designed to produce food for others; although unable to stand, designed to run; although unable to lift a doll, designed to raise a family. We all grow into a potential that was at first incomprehensible to us.

For many people, placing the needs of someone else ahead of their own is as foreign an idea as chewing a carrot is to a toothless tot. Yet just as new teeth push through the gums, the need for commitment and personal fulfillment often drives people to bite off more than they can chew.

In 1858, a small, frail lad was born to a rich family in New York. Along with feeble eyesight, he suffered from asthma so bad that he sometimes couldn't blow out the bedside candle; nevertheless, he became one of the most powerful men on earth.

At eleven or twelve years of age, Theodore Roosevelt's father told him that a good mind alone would not ensure success but that he must build himself a powerful new body to match it. Theodore spent thousands of hours chinning himself, lifting weights, and rattling a punching bag. It's little wonder he rose like a rocket in the world of politics: elected to the New York Legislature at twenty-three; candidate for mayor at twenty-eight; U.S. Civil Service Commissioner under two presidents; president of the police commission of New York; national hero as leader of the Rough Riders in the Spanish-American War at forty; then, in just three busy years, governor of New York, vice president, and president. In 1905 Teddy Roosevelt received the Nobel Peace Prize for his efforts in helping to end the Russo-Japanese War. At five feet nine inches, Roosevelt was a small man, made large through commitment.[3]

Achievement like his may seem beyond our commitment quotient; however, let's not be deceived by what we are. Instead, be challenged by what we are designed to become.

In the early fifteenth century Spain realized it could never compete as a world power with all of its internal rivalries and foreign influences. Spanish leaders designed a commitment that would solidify their country. Two of the most influential and antagonistic families, the Aragones and the Castiles, agreed to end decades of hostility through a planned marriage. In 1479 King Ferdinand II of Aragon and Isabella of Castile united the nation as king and queen. Due to this commitment, the exploits of Christopher Columbus were possible. Later monarchs from this "designed commitment" elevated Spain to an apex of power as the richest and most powerful nation in Europe.[4] As is often the case with human designs and politics, this commitment was not without its subterfuge and strife. But it still illustrates the power behind the reality: Individuals, as well as nations, are designed for commitment.

Other figures of history have met even greater designs. These heroes were committed before birth and by name. God said, "Let us make Adam in our image after our likeness" (Gen. 1:26, KJV). The Hebrew word for "man" in this passage is the name/description *adam* (red mud). Isaac was designed to inherit the promises of God (commitments) even though his mother-to-be had long since passed the age of childbearing. Cyrus of Persia was called by name almost one hundred years before he was sent to fulfill God's comments for Babylon (Isa. 45:1). John the Baptist received his commission before he was conceived (Luke 1:13). And Christ was "foreordained before the foundation of the world" to become our Savior (1 Peter 1:20, KJV).

But what about us today? We live in a time when commitment is not the most popular word in our national vocabulary. The divorce rate continues to climb, while marshals lock up delinquent fathers for nonpayment of support. Personal debt is at an all-time high, while the rate of bank failures is the worst since the Great Depression. We are truly the in-and-out society, where a fad is in one minute and out the next. We even throw things away because it's cheaper than fixing them. Somehow, we feel a commitment to anything will, by definition, be uncomfortable, even painful—too much of a demand on our time, money, or energies.

What are you committed to? Is there *anything* that means *everything* to you? What are you living for? You may respond, "Well, I don't have much time to think about commitment. You see, I've got to get up early every morning, eat breakfast, go to work, come home at six o'clock, have a bite to eat, watch a little TV, go to bed, and that's about it." Or you may say, "There just aren't enough hours in the day for all I want to do. There are friends to see, exciting work to do, games to play, sunsets to watch, children to enjoy, and a big world to understand." Which category do you fit into? Are you somewhere in between?

Even though we are not created just to get by in life, we often give that appearance. Built with the potential for unlimited movement and growth, we seem determined to settle for much less. To seek personal fulfillment and growth, the first clue we discover is one that's obvious to others and obscure to us—YOU. Although perhaps not apparent from your perspective, from the way you look now, or from what you've done before, YOU are part of an unbroken chain of continuous commitments. Designed for commitment, you are the key to the personal fulfillment of yourself and those around you. Anything short of that will diminish the sacrifice and commitment scores of people have already invested in your ability to serve.

24   A Time for Commitment

This key can open the gate to vast new fields of achievement for you. Those who understand the meaning of the game, who have tasted the thrill of victory, who have made the greatest gain now stand ready to help you do the same.

Fritz Kreisler, the great violinist, was approached backstage by an enthusiastic fan who cried, "Mr. Kreisler, I'd give my life to play as you do." "Madame," replied Kreisler, "I did."

2

No Pain ... No Gain

Of all the storytellers in America, I'm still convinced my friend of many years, Art Linkletter, remains one of the best. Here are two true stories Art told recently that underscore the value of commitment. The first one is about an unattractive, scrawny boy from California. As Art tells it,

"He was a sickly ninety-seven-pound high-school boy in San Francisco, so discouraged by his size and continuous bad health that he seldom went out. And no wonder—girls considered him a mess. He wore thick glasses, arch supports, a shoulder brace. Finally he quit high school in complete, total despair about his prospects for a future.

"Then one day, while wandering around in his neighborhood, he attended a health lecture by the late Paul Bragg. The boy was inspired, impressed by the message of hope, and decided he could make some changes in his life.

"So he became a believer in self-determination. He put himself through a rigorous change in lifestyle and diet. He stopped eating junk food, ate nutritious meals, began two hours of daily exercises to strengthen his body. He reentered high school with his newly found confidence.

"Yes, Jack LaLanne was on the road to a brilliant and lucrative career in health programs. He has won many international athletic awards and is even known as Mr. Exercise the world over."[1]

Quite a success story! How did Jack LaLanne do it? He quit feeling sorry for himself, believed that he had the potential for something better, then he acted. That was the key: *He had the courage to act.*

Essentially the same thing happened to another young person in Cedar Rapids, Iowa. Art tells the story of Wendy Stoker, a nineteen-year-old freshman at the University of Florida.

"Last year she placed third, just 2 1/2 points from first, in the Iowa girls' state diving championships. She'd worked two hours a day for four years to get there.

"Now at the University of Florida, she's working twice as hard and has earned the number two position on the varsity diving team, and she's aiming for the national finals. Wendy is carrying a full academic load, finds time for bowling and is an accomplished water-skier.

"But perhaps the most remarkable thing about Wendy Stoker is her typing. She bangs out forty-five words a minute on her typewriter—*with her toes.*

"Oh, did I fail to mention? Wendy was born without arms."[2]

Her gain, too, is the product of commitment.

I mention these stories for two reasons: First, stories of courage, discipline, and commitment are good reminders that we are never stuck in our own situations, regardless of what they may be. What we can conceive and believe, we can achieve. We have choices—the greatest of which is the choice of attitude. Jack LaLanne *chose* to do something about his unimpressive, ninety-seven-pound weakling body. Wendy Stoker *chose* to commit herself to a goal as though she had no disability at all.

Secondly, these stories encourage us to look beyond our own perceived disabilities to the full potential that pulsates within us—that driving force that waits to express itself to the fullest. But the idea of full potential is little more than a hollow phrase until we fill it with gain.

How painful would it be to fall off Mount Everest? That's how Lee Iacocca described his "gut-wrenching" shove from the "grand-hotel suite" office as president of Ford Motor Company to a scruffy transition desk in a company warehouse. He had every reason to give up. He was fifty-four years old, financially secure enough for retirement, and unemployed for the first time in his thirty-two-year career with a single company. Filled with anger, resentment, and humiliation, Iacocca faced a decision.

"There are times in everyone's life when something constructive is born out of adversity. There are times when things seem so bad that you've got to grab your fate by the shoulders and shake it. I was full of anger and I had a simple choice: I could turn that anger against myself, with disastrous results. Or I could take some of that energy and try to do something productive."[3]

Lido Iacocca, the son of an Italian immigrant, then went on to rescue one of America's major auto makers from bankruptcy, pay back an unprecedented federal loan guarantee for one billion dollars seven years early, and rescue 600,000 jobs.

Have you ever grabbed your fate by the shoulders? Shaken it? If not, you can be sure that fate will seize and shake you.

Look at these statements about some super-achievers. "He possesses minimal football knowledge. Lacks motivation," a so-called expert once said of Vince Lombardi. "Can't act! Slightly bald! Can dance a little!" read Fred Astair's first screen test in 1933. Referring to Albert Einstein, someone quipped, "He doesn't wear socks and forgets to cut his hair. Could be mentally retarded." What shield protected them from fate's seizures? Commitment.

I'm convinced that unswerving commitment to a person, a cause, or an idea is the single quality that gives life its vitality. Think how Thomas Edison felt when he dreamed of a lamp that could burn invisible energy. He could have quit, and no one would have blamed him. After all, he had more than ten thousand failures in that one project alone. Chances are you and I haven't had that many failures during all our lifetimes combined.

The Wright brothers wanted to do more than repair bikes in their Dayton, Ohio, bicycle shop, so they dreamed of a machine that could ride the sky. Some laughed at them; others said it was not God's will for men to fly. But Orville and Wilbur determined to follow their dream. On December 17, 1903, near Kitty Hawk, North Carolina, history was made as the first power-driven airplane roared into the sky.

Daniel Webster could not make a speech until after years of disciplined effort but became one of America's greatest orators. George Washington lost more battles than he won but triumphed in the end. Winners never quit, and quitters never win. A cliché, but still true. If you don't believe it, consider these examples.

John Bunyan wrote *Pilgrim's Progress* while languishing in Bedford Prison in England, locked up for his vocal views on religion.

Helen Keller was stricken deaf, blind, and dumb soon after birth. Did she quit? Hardly. Her name already stands alongside those of the most respected people in history. She knew what courage and discipline were all about. We call it commitment.

Charles Dickens began his illustrious career with the unimpressive job of pasting labels on blacking pots. The tragedy of his first love shot through to the depths of his soul, touching off a genius of creativity that made him one of the greatest authors of all time.

Robert Burns was an illiterate country boy; O. Henry, a criminal and an outcast; Beethoven, deaf; Milton, blind. But once they mastered their own weaknesses and committed themselves to service, they strengthened the soul of all humanity.

Are you prepared to master your own weakness? The three greatest words in the English language for gaining fulfillment are DO IT NOW. Work on your commitments prayerfully. Don't wait. DO IT NOW.

Here's a short list of valuable objectives. How many of these are worth as much to you as the ability to type was to Wendy Stoker, the girl without arms?

GAIN WORTH THE PAIN

- having a healthier, happier marriage
- being more open and understanding with your children
- creating more family times together
- losing weight and getting back into condition

- traveling throughout the United States
- becoming more active in local church or community organizations
- volunteering to help the needy in your community
- attending adult education classes at the local college
- learning to play a new sport
- becoming a foster grandparent to orphaned children or to youngsters who have no grandparents

I'm sure you've already thought of other categories. Perhaps now would be a good time to lay this book aside for a few minutes to expand that list. Let your thoughts run free. Make your list of potential commitments as long as possible. Then, take some time to write your objectives in order of their priority. You'll be amazed how much this will reveal about your interests, your desires, and your opportunities.

Then, *act.*

Ultimately, we become the people we choose to be. Although we live together, each of us grows alone. What are we willing to exact from ourselves? It's been said that we're all self-made individuals; however, *only the successful will admit it!*

What's the opposite of no pain . . . no gain? Can we slump back into complacency, assuming we won't get hurt if we don't strive for gain? Unfortunately, no gain . . . *more* pain is true as well. Consider this warning from an unknown poet.

> I bargained with Life for a penny,
>   And Life would pay no more,
> However I begged at evening,
>   When I counted my scanty store.
>
> For Life is a just employer,
>   He gives you what you ask,
> But once you have set the wages,
>   Why, you must bear the task.
>
> I worked for a menial's hire,
>   Only to learn, dismayed,
> That any wage I had asked of Life,
>   Life would have willingly paid.

Are you wasting your life on mere pennies? To what gain are you committing your pain? Hopefully, to something great and wonderful—something larger than yourself. Are you prepared to commit the courage and discipline necessary to make your dreams come true? I hope so. If you're not, you're missing the greatest thrill of all.

Too difficult? Too many obstacles? Too much hard work? We've never hinted that a life of commitment would be easy. But it will be rewarding. Jesus Christ—the One who endured the pain of death to gain your life and mine, the One who looks us straight in the eye and sees beyond our infirmities to the ultimate potential—He is still able to tell us, "All things are possible to those who believe."

Do you believe? If you do, it's going to change your life.

> Everything should be made as simple as possible, but not simpler.
>
> A. Einstein

3

Rules of the Tools

The Greeks recognized an ancient god called Prometheus. He was such a divine trickster that he could change into any person he chose to be. Over time, however, Prometheus transformed into so many different roles, he eventually forgot who he was.[1]

We've examined the value of committing our energy to people and causes far beyond ourselves. We've seen the stirring examples of ordinary people who achieved extraordinary results, taking off the straight jacket labeled "mine" and putting on the mantle labeled "ours." How can we don garments marked "ours" consistently without suffering the same fate as Prometheus?

Let's examine the rules of commitment that prevent us from becoming a paper-cup champion—someone who waits in line, is filled for a moment, and then crushed forever. True commitment renews and regenerates us for each successive challenge.

Picture a telephone technician, complete with leather tool belt, pole-climbing leg irons, and service truck. Just as this professional must understand the rules of these tools, so we must understand the rules of our tools for commitment.

Here's an inventory of important tools and how they operate.

TOOLS FOR COMMITMENT

1. Work Authorization Form. Check for approval and scheduling before making any commitments.
2. Gloves. Don't expect them to keep your hands clean, just free from cuts and abrasions.
3. Safety Goggles. Beware of flying sparks and blinding egos. Some goggles magnify for detail; others give wide angle overviews. Avoid rose-colored shades.
4. Wire Cutters. Make new connections and repair old ones. Note: Never cut off a commitment for taking more than it gives. Add a new line of understanding.
5. Drill. Create the shortest and most efficient route possible for each wire.

6. Soldering Iron. Prepare all surfaces carefully and make sure you don't short out other connections. Fuse wires together.

7. Voltage Tester. Troubleshoot the lines of a commitment to make sure they're connected. Check for dangerous voltage before changing connections. Test your tester on a regular basis. Numerous utility workers have perished from faulty test equipment. Leave nothing to assumption.

8. Screwdriver. Keep things securely bound together. Use it carefully. When taking things apart, look for places that are attached and remove them gently.

9. Amplifier and Filter. Boost weak signals and filter out unwanted noise. Even a good connection will deliver bad results if the sound is garbled.

10. Telephone Hand Set. Transmits only the words that other people expect you to keep. Caution: Never picks up more than you suspect. Hears emotions as well as information.

11. First Aid Kit. Keep nearby for prompt attention. Report all injuries to your supervisor.

12. Pen or Pencil. Document your work. Either you, a co-worker, your boss, or the user will have to answer for this commitment.

Though this list is whimsical, it still represents some important concepts. How many of them can you identify in actual use? As we recount the story of a young man's commitment to himself and his family, see how many of these tools you recognize *in action.*

When historians tell of the distance runner who finally broke the barrier of the four-minute mile, they also give credit to a crippled athlete who came within 4.5 seconds of the same goal, sixteen years earlier. The story of Glenn Cunningham and his powerful legs can make your knees grow weak with astonishment.

At the age of seven, Glenn Cunningham was injured by an explosion that killed his brother and engulfed his own legs in flames. Doctors declared he would never walk again. But he and his mother refused to submit to discouragement and self-pity. They massaged the muscles in his twisted legs for hours on end, month after month. When he set aside his crutches after three years, the doctors cautioned him not to expect too much. Glenn still limped when he entered high school. But after four years of iron determination on the track team, Glenn was awarded an athletic scholarship by the University of Kansas. The same miracle of spirit that reached back to heal his shriveled sinew now threw him forward into victory after victory.

Cunningham captured the world record for the mile in 1934 at 4:06.7 seconds. People who had never taken an interest in track events became fascinated by his endeavors. Almost every race was headline news. In 1938, Glenn Cunningham stunned the world with his scarred and deformed legs. He sliced the official record down to 4:04.4.

Authorities had calculated that the human heart would never withstand the strain of four four-minute miles in a row. But a twenty-seven-year-old athlete with a disability achieved ninety-eight percent of this unachievable goal. What should a normal runner be able to do? It took another sixteen years for Roger Bannister, an Englishman, to complete this assault on the impossible. How much of his victory can be attributed to the commitment of a crippled youngster who refused to give up?[2]

How many tools did you find? From filtering out words of discouragement to wearing out several pairs of work gloves, I saw Glenn Cunningham handling the tools of commitment with skill and confidence. Can you see yourself doing the same? To make it possible for you to break through your own private four-minute barriers, let's examine a few more fundamentals of commitment.

I've heard it said, "If you don't know where you're going, you'll probably wind up someplace else." How true. You can't bowl without pins; you can't play golf without greens and holes; and you can't shoot basketball without a net. Yet how many of us try to wander through life without direction? Is every wind an ill wind to the sailor with no destination? Maybe there's some value to not setting goals.

FIVE REASONS TO IGNORE GOAL SETTING

1. Friends can find you a lot faster when you're stuck in one place.
2. Co-workers won't have any trouble getting ahead of someone who's wandering in circles.
3. It's easier to procrastinate when there's less to put off.
4. Having no money saves time at the bank.
5. We can stop our list here. People without any goals don't count much anyway.

Other people have the opposite problem—more goal than coal to fire it. "Too many commitments amount virtually to none," says Elton Trueblood in *The Company of the Committed.* That's like the adolescent boy who buys twenty valentines that say, "To my one and only. . . ." That's a sure invitation to a massive "heart" attack. To achieve the right balance in goal setting, use another important tool of commitment—communication.

DON'T TRIP OVER THE CORD

The harder some people try to communicate, the more they trip all over themselves. Why? The following points, developed for an audio-cassette seminar entitled *Cornerstones of Communication,* show how communication consists of a cord with at least five separate strands.[3] If you overlook any one of these, you'll not only weaken the entire cord but also leave dangerous loose ends. Let's examine these strands.

Strand #1—Transmitter, the source of your message. "Good job" coming from a new trainee has much less power than those same words transmitted by the boss.

Strand #2—Receptor, your intended audience. Make sure you're fully connected before communicating. If you don't call the audience to attention, they'll never salute your idea.

Strand #3—Message, your formal communication. The real meaning of any message lies in the interpretation your audience places on the idea, not in the words alone. If a wealthy woman from Beverly Hills hears "This is cheap," she'll never buy one. But if a housewife in the inner city with five kids hears "This is cheap," she'll probably buy a dozen. Compose your message for results, not just content.

Strand #4—Channel, the pathway of your message. Should you deliver your idea in writing, over the phone, in person, or some other way? A spoken thank you is appreciated at the moment, but recognition in the newspaper is remembered for months to come. Look for the most appropriate channel.

Strand #5—Time, both time of day and number of repetitions in a message. Which of these two messages creates more anxiety? A phone call from your friend at 5:30 in the afternoon requesting an immediate ride home or a phone call from your friend at 11:30 in the evening requesting an immediate ride home? The message is identical except for the element of time. And if it's the third time today you've received this call, you'd become even more anxious.

Braided together, these five strands of communication form a cord that will help you bind any commitment. Now that you're developing productive commitments, how do you maintain them long enough to bring about personal fulfillment? For some, the answer is courage.

As a youngster, Arthur Mitchell was told he couldn't dance professionally. He not only grew up to be a dancer but opened a school with an international reputation for helping children from the ghetto entertain the elite.

Here's how it happened. Young Mitchell was a good social dancer in junior high. A teacher suggested he apply to a high school for the performing arts. But after they accepted him, "They told me I'd never be a dancer and that I should go into another profession." Viewing this as a challenge, Mitchell determined to become a classical ballet dancer when Blacks were rarely members of ballet companies.

Through courage and perseverance, Mitchell made a name for himself. But he still wasn't satisfied. Remembering the needs of all the city youngsters back home, he said to himself, *Arthur, get out there and do something—teach them to dance.*[4] Thus began the Dance Theater of Harlem.

For others, the key to lasting commitment is persistence. Examine the history of this winner disguised as a loser who just wouldn't quit.

THE WINNER IN DISGUISE

Lost his job in 1832
Was defeated for the legislature in 1832
Failed in business in 1833
Lost his sweetheart to death in 1835
Had a nervous breakdown in 1836
Was defeated for Speaker in 1838
Was defeated in bid for Congress in 1843
Was elected to Congress in 1846
Lost nomination bid for Congress in 1848
Was rejected for Land Officer in 1849
Was defeated for Senate in 1854
Lost nomination for Vice Presidency in 1856
Was again defeated for Senate in 1858
Was elected our 16th president in 1860

I leave you with an eight-word rule from the Master of commitment, Jesus Christ. He who changed water into wine, raised the dead, and walked out of the garden tomb reminds all of us, "I can of my own self do nothing" (John 5:30, KJV). The ultimate power is from God Himself.

Persistence, courage, goals, communication— these qualities can thrust your life into high orbit. Only God can maintain the life support system. Billions of people have died in search of these life-giving principles. I wish I could say that the mere act of reading this chapter would guarantee your success. That's unrealistic. But I can guarantee that if you'll begin to apply these rules—not once but maybe as often as you breathe in and breathe out—then you *will* cultivate effective commitments. The opportunity and the promise are there *if* you will put these rules into practice. And if you'd like to know where you might go to practice them, I invite you to knock on the door of part two.

Part 2

Does The House Next Door Have a Neighbor?

When your neighbor's house is afire, your own property is at stake.

Horace

Coming together is a beginning,
Staying together is progress,
Working together is success.

                                Anonymous

4

"Who Is My Neighbor?"

In *The Great Divorce*, C. S. Lewis describes a
fictional hell where the people are so quarrelsome
that they continually move further and further
away from each other. One resident of hell ex-
plains it this way, "The trouble is that they're so
quarrelsome. As soon as anyone arrives, he settles
in some street. Before he's been there twenty-four
hours, he quarrels with his neighbor. Before the
week is over, he's quarreled so badly that he
decides to move. Very soon he finds the next street
empty because all the people there have quarreled
with their neighbors—and moved."[1]

That, of course, is fiction. Most neighborhoods

are packed beyond capacity. The buildings are close together, but what about the people inside? Haven't they moved apart in thought and action?

People today live in several different places at once. Besides home, there's the office, the club, school, church, and elsewhere. Each with our own set of neighbors, we're often closer to someone several towns away who shares an office than we are to the family next door whose sprinkler we have to dodge.

WHO, THEN, IS OUR NEIGHBOR?

A sly manipulator posed this same question to Jesus Christ after he was admonished to "love your neighbor as yourself." In reply, Christ expounded the parable of the good Samaritan and asked the lawyer which man he thought was neighbor to the crime victim. The lawyer answered, "He who showed mercy on him." Christ added, "Go and do likewise."

This seems clear enough from our perspective two thousand years later. But we've got to understand the background of a Samaritan to fully appreciate the edge on this answer. Jews of that day would not even speak to Samaritans, who were despised as a heathen minority brought in to occupy northern Palestine by the Assyrians when they conquered the Israelites seven centuries earlier. Besides being "inferior Gentiles," these Samaritans were squatters, totally unwelcomed by the Jews as neighboring citizens. Animosity, anger, and violence were commonplace. How could a socialite Jew be expected to serve this race "as yourself"?

Here's a modern comparison. Think of telling a prominent lawyer from Washington D.C. to invite an undocumented alien or a gang member out to lunch. How well would that be accepted?

Richard Valdemar remembers a high-school friend who vowed he would return and build a better neighborhood at home in the barrios of Los Angeles. "He went off to Yale and got a law degree and became a big success, but he didn't live up to that promise." Richard had made that same vow himself but came back. He is now a member of an elite county sheriff unit that helps violent street gangs avoid trouble. Though he earns less than he could make in private industry, Richard Valdemar's only regret is that so many who leave the poor Hispanic neighborhoods have no feeling for those who remain.[2]

Life at the girls' school in India was fulfilling enough until Agnes Bojaxhiu received "the message" in 1946. "Quit the cloistered existence and plunge into Calcutta's slums," declared the vision. Thus began a crusade that earned a Nobel Peace Prize in 1979 for Mother Teresa. From collecting abandoned babies out of the garbage to building leprosariums, the Missionaries of Charity are committed to serving others "as yourself." The order functions worldwide with 1800 nuns, 250 brothers, and thousands of co-workers in thirty countries. What compels a neighbor like this?

"For me each one is an individual," Mother Teresa once explained. "It is not social work. We must love each other. It involves emotional involvement, making people feel they are wanted."[3]

Hazel Hudson saw a need and filled it. In 1972, parents in a Black neighborhood in Chicago were concerned about the growing number of youth gangs. So, a local church opened a private school for youngsters, but they needed a principal. Although Hazel had only served as a community representative for the Chicago Public Schools, she was picked for the job. Hazel returned to college and poured herself into the task for twelve to fourteen hours a day. Over the years, she turned down many offers for jobs well above her salary of $21,000. "This is my life—working with people and caring about them and watching people grow."[4]

It's easy to look at glowing examples like these and feel overwhelmed. People remark, "I could never do anything like that" or "I don't have anything to offer." Perhaps, they're right today; nevertheless, the only sure constant in life is change. We've already seen how we are designed for commitment. Like a young girl wondering what kind of profile she'll make in a sweater some day, maybe your commitment hasn't fully developed yet. But sights of the present must not block our vision for the future.

I have seen people make the mistake of spending so much time packing for that one big mission in life that they never know when the boat loads up and leaves. Commitments start small and grow bigger. What we need is an ongoing program of small commitments that prepares us for the big opportunities to come. Let's examine a few exercises that will build your commitment quotient day by day.

COMMITMENT WARM-UPS

Exercise #1: Meet someone new each week. How would you feel if one of the officers, directors, or chief executives stopped to express interest in you and your projects? We all long for attention. Now look around at all the people who look up to you and seek recognition from "the higher-ups." What enormous power you hold in your hand if you'll only recognize someone down the line! Nothing makes a group of people more supportive than an occasional beam of attention and praise. Commit yourself to meet someone new or recognize someone's accomplishments at least *once* each week. Schedule this if you have to.

Exercise #2: Smile: Commit yourself to one conscious smile every day, even if it's self-conscious. Hold time and motion in thick molasses for a moment while I describe what happens during one deliberate smile.

Smiler (one who gives a smile): *There goes a member of my team. I appreciate the value of your presence and want you to know that our relationship (commitment) is ready to function now!*

Smilee (one who receives the smile): *Hey, that person knows who I am, why I'm here, what I need, and what I can contribute. And they seem to appreciate it all! Maybe we can get something done here.*

Now take a moment to consider the opposite effects of a frown.

Exercise #3: Open with Care: A friend of mine tells the story about hearing a soft knock at the back door. Being a teenager at the time, he leaped up, jerked open the inside door, and thrust out the screen with the grace of a rodeo gate. No one in sight. Who had knocked? Then from the side of the three-foot porch came the voice of a tiny youngster who had been swept aside by the onrushing door. The teen felt small enough to pass through the screen, but the damage was already done. How many times have you seen someone open a door in the face of some unfortunate victim on the other side? Or bolt through a doorway so fast that he collides with someone else in the hallway?

Because all of us have a commitment to unseen travelers on the far side of a doorway, here's a lesson in *How to open a door without knocking down the rest of the world.*

1. Unlatch the handle with enough snap to warn any nearby pet, child, or off-balance traveler that his life may be in immediate peril.
2. Wait 117.5 nanoseconds (or 1 blink if you

have trouble counting in billionths of a second).

3. Smoothly open the door and step into the stream of foot traffic, which you presume to be coming.

Beware of these seemingly simple exercises. The main principle behind them is a matter of life and limb and at the heart of defensive driving, Red Cross preparedness, and self-help groups. Do not dismiss them lightly. Practice these simple commitments and you will esteem the comfort and safety of others equal to or greater than your own.

Who is your neighbor? I submit that it's anyone beyond the next door, anyone who could use a smile, anyone in need of a Good Samaritan.

In the words of Bob Gibson, a cardiologist from Portland, Oregon, who has worked as a pediatrician with our World Vision relief efforts in Ethiopia: "For me, this is an opportunity to fulfill all the things I thought about when I started medical school. Here, you really feel useful. What you do makes a difference, a tremendous difference."5

After explaining the importance of serving commoners "as yourself," Jesus gave us another parable, "You have been faithful over a few things, I will make you ruler over many things." (Matt. 25:21, NIV). What's it worth to your neighbor for you to be faithful over a few small commitments? What's it worth to you? You might be surprised.

> If I'd known I was going to live this long, I woulda taken better care of myself.
>
> Jimmy Durante

5

Surprised by Joy

I smile every time I think of those profound words spoken by entertainer Jimmy Durante. I suppose we all feel that way at one time or another. "If I'd only known . . ." Many neighbors actually rely upon us. How often do we say, "If only someone would have told me . . . if I'd just had that insight?" If, if, if . . .

Let's suppose for a moment this is your last day on earth. You have been asked to reflect long and hard on your life, your job, your interests, and your relationship to your friends, to your family, to God, and to your church and then to talk about your life's priorities. What would you say? Would you paraphrase Durante's words by lamenting, "If I'd known I was going to live this long, I would have been more serious about my commitments?" Or would you be able to close your eyes for the last time, feeling content, ready to say good-by?

I've heard it said that you're not really ready for life until you know what you want to say when you're dead, that is, on your tombstone. That's an interesting idea to pursue for a moment. You fill in the blanks. "Here lies _____, known for his/her commitments to _____.

If this is truly what you are committed to, how are you doing? How did you do yesterday? What has been your progress today? A friend of mine has a little slogan on her desk that asks, Is what you are about to do bringing you closer to your goal? I ask you the same question about your commitments.

Earlier, we talked about the pain and discipline needed for a productive commitment. We noted how people like Helen Keller, Thomas Edison, John Bunyan, the Wright Brothers, and others struggled through what seemed like insurmountable odds in pursuit of their commitment and ultimate success. In this chapter, we'll look at some of the payoffs that come our way when we burn the destructive fortresses of hesitation, half-baked enthusiasm, and lethargy, and instead build bridges of decision, excitement, perseverance, and single-minded commitment.

I'm afraid too many see commitment as drudgery—something that will cramp their style and keep them from having a good time. Many people want the results of commitment; however, most are unwilling to pay the price. Like a man from Texas once remarked, "Preacher, you've done quit the preaching and gone to meddlin'."

Why are we so eager to improve our circumstances, but so reluctant to improve our lives? Some say, "I'm too young to get all worked up and committed to anything!" Still others say, "I'm over the hill . . . time is no longer on my side." Benjamin Franklin didn't seem to have that problem. He was eighty-one years old when he helped create the Constitution of the United States; at sixteen, a newspaper columnist. The great Mozart was seven years old when he published his first composition. George Bernard Shaw was a crusty ninety-four when one of his plays had its first performance. William Pitt was in his mid-twenties when he became prime minister of Great Britain; Golda Meir, seventy-one when she was elected prime minister of Israel. No one is too old or too young to make a significant contribution. Age has absolutely no bearing on ability. You and I can choose to live a life of commitment at any time with an attitude that says *I can and I will.* There are simply no more excuses. Period! ˙ Look at this profound message.

> If you think you are beaten, you are.
> If you think you dare not, you don't.
> If you like to win, but you think you can't,
> It is almost certain you won't.

If you think you'll lose, you're lost.
For out of the world we find,
Success begins with a person's will—
It's all in the state of mind.

If you think you're outclassed, you are,
You've got to think high to rise,
You've got to be sure of yourself before
You can ever win a prize.

Life's battles don't always go
To the stronger woman or man,
But sooner or later the one who wins,
Is the one WHO THINKS "I CAN!"

Dorothy McKinney was content to remain a practical nurse at Miami's Jackson Memorial Hospital. But after seven years on the job, her co-workers recognized something better. They encouraged Dorothy to enter training and become a registered nurse. "I was just doing a job, but others saw potential," she says. "My cocky attitudes changed toward being able to help somebody." With that encouragement, Dorothy was surprised to become supervisor of the orthopedics and neurology sections, to receive the 1983 Outstanding Nurse Award, and to be interviewed for a national magazine.[1]

The greatest literary artist in American history and one of our foremost novelists, Nathaniel Hawthorne, not only owed his success to the daily inspiration of his wife, but also to his only opportunity to compose first his mind, then his masterpiece. If it had not been for Sophia, perhaps we would not remember Nathaniel. After he lost his job in the customhouse, he went home a broken-hearted man to tell his wife that he was a failure. To his amazement, she beamed with joy and said, "Now you can write your book!" When he bitterly responded, "Yes, and what shall we live on while I am writing it?" the astounding woman opened a drawer and took out a mysterious hoard of cash. "Where on earth did you get that?" he gasped. "I have always known that you were a man of genius. I knew that some day you would write an immortal masterpiece. So every week, out of the money you have given me for housekeeping, I have saved something; there is enough to last us one whole year." Thoroughly surprised, Hawthorne sat down and wrote one of the finest literary pieces in the Western Hemisphere—*The Scarlet Letter.*[2]

Once you have rightly directed your attitude, the possibilities are endless for living out the joy that soars on a life of commitment.

RESULTS YOU CAN SEE

The first, and perhaps most obvious, result of our commitment to a loving God is *personal growth.* It's been said that God's reward for a job well done is to give us a bigger job to do. Similarly, commitment, even at its struggling, most fledgling level, contributes to personal growth and enhances our capacity to grow even more.

Internal peace that results from decision is

another by-product of commitment. Be hot or
cold, not in between because there is no peace in
indecision. Someone once said, "On the beach of
hesitation bleach the bones of countless millions
who sat down to wait and waiting, died." Ever
wonder why the big fish vomited Jonah? The
disobedient preacher was *lukewarm!* Commitment and lukewarmness fly in the face of each
other; commitment and a deep sense of internal
peace go hand in hand.

When you commit yourself to God and to His
plans, there is yet a third result. *Your life takes on
purpose.* You discover a reason for living. Suddenly, you are more than flesh and bone. You are a
person of destiny and purpose, echoing these
words of the poet Goethe, "Knowing is not
enough; we must apply. Willing is not enough; we
must do." Then, you begin to *do it* with an
enthusiasm and desire you never had before.
Why? Because you are living your God-ordained
design for commitment. You are making commitment work for you.

The pleasure you gain from action is intimately
tied to your level of service to others. I like what
my friend Charles "Tremendous" Jones says,
"Work as hard as you can, get as much as you can,
give as much as you can." That's happiness.
That's fulfillment.

Often, people say, "I'm unhappy," as if happiness were somehow supposed to be the ultimate
purpose of life. I've found just the opposite.
Usually I'm happiest when I'm not even thinking

about being happy. Happiness and joy are always by-products of my commitment to a task, a person, or an idea, often in the midst of intense struggle—even pain. But without question, my greatest happiness comes in service to others and in my commitment to projects, people, and plans bigger than myself.

SPIRIT JOY

For the follower of Jesus Christ, there is no end to the service we can provide to those around us. It makes no difference how old we are, where we live, or the state of our physical health. *There are simply no excuses for not living a life of commitment to what is worthy, honest, and just.* But it's not something we dare do with our own strength alone. Secular humanism continues to be the underlying philosophy of the world today; nevertheless, this system cannot endure. We need a divine Savior every day. Once our commitment to Jesus Christ is secure, then and only then are we ready to receive the greatest joys imaginable. It's as true today as it was for the people who needed that loving touch from the Man of Galilee more than two thousand years ago.

"These things have I spoken to you, that my joy might remain in you, and that your joy might be full." (John 15:11, KJV). The joy that He experienced in serving the world of His day is waiting for us today.

It takes two people to make one brother.

Israel Zangwill

6

Family and Other Strangers

I challenge you to define "family" outside the realm of commitment. A young child might say, "A family is everybody in one home." But what about Aunt Elizabeth who lives down South? Or that student away from home? An older child might guess, "Family is everyone with the same last name." But that doesn't allow for the mother's maiden name. An adolescent might offer the concept of blood lines and race. But that doesn't account for the whole branch of maternal lineage of any ancestry. Therefore, we conclude that a family cannot exist, so the Hatfields and the McCoys can quit their feuding.

People give birth to a family when they make the *commitment* to share their home, their name, and their blood. This commitment must be continually ratified in body, mind, and spirit if the family is to survive. This understanding is as rich in symbolism as it is expensive in responsibility.

We talk of being married to a project or having brain children and soul brothers. That's all very good *if* we are continually nourishing our commitments to those living relationships with parents, family, spouse, and church.

There are sires who do not "father." There are women who give birth who do not "mother." Conversely, there are foster parents who become "mom" and "dad" and engender the potential for grandchildren. The whole concept of family is as flighty as butterflies in the wind. But if we lose sight of those higher relationships in family, we're well on the road to the lower instincts of animals.

The most common commitment is the marriage vow: ". . . till death do us part." All too often, it lasts until discontent do us part. A marriage counselor once observed, "What married people don't realize is that single people are unhappy too—they just don't have anyone to blame it on." Ernest D. Lawson added, "Fifty years ago, parents were apt to have a lot of kids. Nowadays kids are apt to have a lot of parents."

Look at the frightful statistics. Nearly one out of two marriages ends in divorce. Half the homicides committed are within the family—the very unit that was designed to create and nurture life. Most kidnapping and abduction is done by parents taking child-custody litigation into their own hands. If family is the womb of civilization, much of the world is seeking a global abortion. What should our families be like? How can you move toward greater happiness and fulfillment with your loved ones?

Successful marriage requires falling in love many times, always with the same person. When the late Mr. and Mrs. Henry Ford celebrated their golden wedding anniversary, a reporter asked them, "To what do you attribute your fifty years of successful married life?" "The formula," said Ford, "is the same formula I have always used in making cars—just stick to one model."

In 1821, Elizabeth Barrett, the precocious English poet, fell from a pony and was rendered an invalid at fifteen. Having reconciled herself to a quiet life of solitude, she continued producing superior verse till the age of forty when she was swept off her feet by someone else's commitment. Six years her junior and another accomplished poet of the land, Robert Browning looked at an invalid woman but saw a carefree girl. Their romance and marriage of twenty-one years inspired both poets to produce their most memorable works.[1] One of her poems, bearing his last name, captures the essence of commitment to others.[2]

REWARD OF SERVICE

The sweetest lives are those to duty wed,
Whose deeds both great and small
Are close-knit strands of an unbroken thread,
Where love ennobles all . . .
A poor man served by thee shall make thee rich;
A sick man helped by thee shall make thee
    strong;
Thou shalt be served thyself by every sense
Of service which thou renderest.

One pastor tells of an elderly couple who were deeply devoted to each other. When his wife died, the husband became listless and lost all will to live. The pastor mentioned to the husband the valuable deed he was performing for his wife. If he had died first, she would have been all alone in the world. Now he is able to bear that grief and loneliness in her place. This understanding restored dignity and meaning to his life.

These examples give a glimpse of what can take place in a family rich with commitment. But what can be done for those families who need greater deposits of commitment?

Not too long ago, I let a few friends and associates talk me into a grueling experience. They felt my background of more than forty years with Dorothy, our sons and daughter, cherished friends, colleagues, and associates might make an inspiring book called *The Fine Art of Friendship.* I've written a number of books in my career ranging from management of people and time to motivation and excellence. But they were mostly about someone else. This book, however, would hit pretty close to home. How could I help other people make friends and become a friend without getting into some rather personal stories? I couldn't talk about them without talking about me as well.

So I wrestled with these questions: Should I skip the topic, try to hoodwink everyone into thinking my friends and I live with Snow White, or should I disclose some of the coarse ingredients about Ted Engstrom that are refined into the fine art of friendship?

As you suspect by now, I bit the bullet and continue to dodge occasional ricochets. With my personal example, I am underscoring the value of one of the most important principles to strengthen your family—open communication.

There were a great deal of happy stories I was eager to relate in the book; however, I also explained how Dorothy and I reacted to the news that our twenty-one-year-old son was using marijuana. I'm not proud to say it happened in my family, especially since I am an evangelist of the Word. But I am pleased to say that Gordon gave me cause to reevaluate and strengthen a number of important values. We have a great relationship today (and we could have had it sooner without the pot if my head had been a little clearer). I also retraced steps over some sharp stone pathways between myself and the founder of World Vision. Once again, I'm pleased to report that with the encouragement of other close friends, our relationship improved and was strengthened.

Communicate openly. Talk about your problems and listen to your friends. From Roger Golde's *What You Say Is What You Get,* here are a few more ways to strengthen your commitment to the family.[3]

GIVING TOLERABLE CRITICISM

1. To give criticism is to remove something (esteem, self-worth). Leave an escape hatch: "In my opinion . . . ," "The way I see it . . . ," "Sometimes . . . ," "Possibly . . ."

2. Criticize the idea or opinion, not the person. Dangerous: "You don't think things through very carefully." Safer: "I see some inconsistencies in your position."

3. Limit criticism to one thing at a time, then limit your total to two or three.

4. Follow a specific criticism with "Therefore . . . ," "So . . . ," "As a result . . ." This allows people to understand your objection better.

5. End criticism by restating the problem or suggesting alternatives and their benefit. This returns something to the person from whom your criticism took esteem.

Golde develops another valuable point about criticism that I'll call Rule Zero. It needs to come first. If you ignore it, you've just multiplied all your other efforts by zero.

0. If you can't bring something positive to mind

about the other person, postpone your criticism. You cannot criticize other people effectively, especially in your own family, without first criticizing yourself. If you can't find something of value in the actions of another person, then one of you is an idiot, and the rest of your actions are merely a contest to see who it is.

WHY BOTHER WITH FATHER?

The root of strong family ties is fatherhood. Couples who understand the role of his father and her father are far better equipped to understand the role of their children's father.

An acquaintance of mine was feeling somewhat forlorn while away on a business trip. His relationship with his father back home wasn't all he wanted it to be, and his two youngsters at home were going three days without their daddy. Four hundred miles from the children and twelve hundred miles from Dad, he sat down in a lonely hotel room and penned these words.

THE SON'S PRAYER

Our Father who lives back home,
We uphold your name.
Let your family expand.
Let your ways be done wherever we go,
Even as they are at your home.
Give us today what we need the most.
And forgive us our mistakes.

Even as we forgive our brothers, sisters &
   friends.
Lead us not into bitter lessons,
But save us from harm.
For your family is the authority,
The strength and the reputation,
For me and my children
And their children's children thereafter.

And so it is . . .

Lee Iacocca pays enormous tribute to the inspiration of his father. He relates in his autobiography, "My father and I were very close. I loved pleasing him, and he was always terrifically proud of my accomplishments. . . . Most of my friends would never hug their fathers. I guess they were afraid of not appearing strong and independent. But I hugged and kissed my dad at every opportunity—nothing could have felt more natural. . . . People say to me, 'You're a roaring success. How did you do it?' I go back to what my parents taught me. Apply yourself! Get all the education you can, but then, by God *do* something! Don't just stand there, make something happen. It isn't easy, but if you keep your nose to the grindstone and work at it, it's amazing how in a free society you can become as great as you want to be."[4]

That determined attitude, nurtured by a father, helped account for the Chrysler turnaround. It can do the same for your family.

In these days of distraction and danger, it's not always easy to stir up our own motivation and commitment. What happens when the phone rings and someone says, "Come quick, it's your father!" or "Mother needs you, something's wrong!" What happens to your commitment? With family, it doesn't even have to be a crisis to catapult us into action. Little triumphs pull the starter cord of commitment: "Hey, Sally had a baby girl"; "Look, Jeff lost another tooth"; "Sandy got straight A's. Let's go celebrate." I wish I could report a few more family occasions to celebrate; however, through my travels and responsibilities at World Vision, I'm more inclined to say, "Come quick, Father needs you. The world family is suffering."

People look at our institution, really any institution composed of humans in the service of God, and ask, "What can such a small group do in the face of such overwhelming odds?" I've learned to answer, "God will provide." His commitment to His family is unmovable.

We talked about how you cannot define "family" apart from commitment. And just as commitment creates the physical family we see and understand, so commitment begets the spiritual family we cannot see. "Whosoever shall do the will of my Father which is in heaven, the same is my brother, and sister, and mother" (Matt. 12:50, KJV).

There's a massive faith-filled army of saints past, present, and future waiting to answer our Father's call for help. I don't know when He's going to mobilize the entire clan. But I do know I want to be there when He does. Meanwhile, there's a lot to be done right here and now.

Part 3

Commitment to a Physical World in Spiritual Need

Those who make peaceful revolution impossible will make violent revolution inevitable.

J.F. Kennedy

> If this revolution is not aimed at changing people, then I'm not interested.
>
> Grafitti on a wall in Havana

7

New Hope
for the Hopeless

Earlier, we examined the *Who* of commitment—your family and your neighbors—and the *How*. Now let's complete the process of discovering your hidden key to personal fulfillment by exploring the *Where, When, What* and *Why* of commitment.

At two-and-a-half-years, Kim Leang weighed only fifteen pounds when his mother brought him into the relief center in Kampuchea. Due to a bout with measles and a vitamin A deficiency, he had lost the vision in his right eye, was lethargic, and could not walk. Tuberculosis and bronchial pneumonia compounded the problems. Kim was only one of several hundred children in that immediate region. That's why World Vision participates with a local project known as Rehydration, Immunization, Nutrition, and Education—R.I.N.E. This was but one of three thousand projects in seventy-seven countries World Vision had the privilege of serving in 1984.

As the president of a global institution, I learn about many problems of staggering proportions. Fortunately, there are regular follow-up reports from youngsters like Kim. Thanks to careful treatment at the R.I.N.E. Center, Kim Leang gained weight and soon began walking and playing. To provide for his continued good health, Kim's mother learned about nutrition and hygiene at the center.

We need to hear these success stories. Ethiopia alone has seven million famine victims with forty-five agencies scrambling to provide assistance. New tragedies and terrors erupt daily in Bangladesh, Lebanon, Central America, urban U.S.A. . . .

What do these massive problems have to do with our own private world? "What can one individual do?" I often hear. Here's a powerful answer.

Lillian Tasher went to Egypt as a young woman around the turn of the century because she believed God wanted her to go there. She did not have the support of a mission agency; she did not even have funds for her passage. She prayed, and someone gave her the money to go to Egypt. Once there, she founded an orphanage in Assuit, which has taken care of thousands of orphans, and was known as "Mama Lillian." Riding a donkey, she begged food from the area farmers to feed her children. Because of her, many Egyptian children grew up to be Christians.

"Missionaries are simply a bunch of nobodies trying to exalt Somebody," said Jim Elliot, a missionary who was killed during his attempt to reach the Auca Indians in 1956. Are you a nobody? What can you do? Nothing of your own self, according to John 5:30. Through the power of God, Christ conquered the grave; through the power of God, Jim Elliot's example has inspired untold hundreds, perhaps thousands, of volunteers to serve a thousandfold more people. Both examples continue to bear fruit today. God provides new hope for the hopeless by adding new servants to the family, one at a time.

HOW ONE ADDS UP

I am only one, but I *am* one;
I cannot do everything
But I can do something.
What I can do, I ought to do
And what I ought to do
By the grace of God, I *will* do.
Canon Farrar

EVIDENCE OF THINGS NOT SEEN

"I don't believe in anything I can't see!" people sometimes tell me. I have to smile and ask them if they can see air, electricity, or microwaves. We're forced to believe in things we cannot see. Paul tells us that faith is "the evidence of things *not seen*" (Heb. 11:1, KJV). The working of the Spirit through faith is invisible, but real. We discern it by the effects.

Two boys nearly caused an accident with nothing more than spirit. They placed themselves on both sides of a busy avenue and stretched an imaginary rope across the road. Tensing themselves in a tug-of-war posture, they convinced the oncoming driver that the path was blocked by a strong cord. He slammed on the brakes, skidded sideways, and sent up a plume of tire burns. Unfortunately, the spirit world is real. We need to oppose the spirits of destruction and cling to the Spirit of life.

All of us are writing a story *in spirit* on the tablets of our heart—a story that might be shouted from the housetops someday (Luke 12:2, 3). There's nothing done in secret that will not be revealed. Even our most intimate thoughts leave bold impressions on the Book of Life. Some of Christ's family members are writing epic chapters of service.

"Even if you're surrounded by children who are going to die, you can share kindness, water, food, medical care. In a way, we're doing what the Lord would do if He was here. He has given me a very special love for these people." The life of Carolyn Kippenberger, a nurse from New Zealand serving in Ethiopia, is an example of faith that was not lost on a few dying children. Instead it gave new hope to hundreds of fellow victims by strengthening their commitment to live. In 1985, the *Los Angeles Times* reported her inspiring work in the same issue that featured World Vision worker Elizabeth Budd.[1] My heart was overjoyed to see this "evidence of things not seen" in print.

"You can't see commitment," writes Art Williams in the *Saturday Evening Post.* "You can only see the results. But then, what difference does it make? When you have it, you know it's there. So will everyone else."[2]

SUBSTANCE OF THINGS HOPED FOR

Not only is faith the "evidence of things not seen," it is also the "substance of things *hoped for*" (Heb. 11:1, KJV). When a volunteer from the Western world leaves a comfortable job, car, community, and home to work from dawn to dusk, sleep in tents or sheds, eat *injara* (a pancake made from grain), and work with little more than bare hands, he or she is relying upon the "substance of things hoped for." When a dazed disaster victim accepts the guidance of an outsider and gives up old ideas to implement new suggestions in food, medicine, clothing, housing, transportation, and other cherished habits, that's the "substance of things hoped for." What can an awareness of faith and vision do for you? It can unlock the power of faith in your life—faith that will sustain your commitments through wind and rain, storm and flood.

Please *don't* read this as a recruiting drive for World Vision. We would be hard pressed to train and outfit everyone if you did. Please *do* read this as a call for commitment to those in need near you. Loss of a loved one is the same for all skin colors; financial problems can strike in any currency; natural disasters don't consult a map; illness doesn't look up names; and a cry means the same in every language. What we're doing in seventy-seven countries, you can do in seventy-seven households, if not in deeds or dollars, at least in prayers.

We need a converted Karl Marx! Or a healed Hitler! Or Alexander the Righteous! Commitment gone mad is no excuse to get mad at commitment. For reasons too profound for me to explain, it appears to the human eye that the odds are running 10,000 to 1 in favor of the Adversary. But somehow, I don't think God is leaving all that much to chance. The "evidence of things not seen" and "substance of things hoped for" are too compelling. God still loves the world, and Christ is at His side with even greater power and authority.

God and Christ are doing their part to prepare new hope for the hopeless. Are we doing ours? Many people yearn to do something fulfilling with their lives, but they feel restrained. If you've experienced that frustration, examine the freedom of slavery in the next chapter.

Pressed into service means
pressed out of shape.

Robert Frost

8

The Freedom
of Slavery

Our world is slave to a cruel taskmaster. He
gives us a great deal of freedom but exacts
enormous tribute. Let's look at some other task-
masters.

The automobile allows us to go almost anywhere
we choose. All it asks in return is fifty thousand
lives *each year*. That price tag is the same as *ten
years* in Vietnam! Perhaps we should construct a
memorial the size of the one for Vietnam veterans
in Washington for those fallen highway comrades
each year!

Examine entertainment. We have the freedom
to choose from a world of magazines, books,

games, theme parks, theater, movies, television, and on and on the list goes. So does the tribute required by their master. It is now estimated that preschoolers spend more time in front of the television than it takes to earn a college degree. Their grades and behavior reflect this priority. Recently, a world-cup soccer match in Belgium erupted into a bloody free-for-all. Thirty-eight people died when *fan*atics from Liverpool flew into a mindless rage so out of control that officials *had* to allow the game to be played for fear of more bloodshed. Free people should have silently disbanded in shame and immediately planned some type of memorial service. But their master wouldn't let them.

We could discuss the freedom of credit with its multitrillion dollar price tag, including the U.S. deficit and the personal debt we individuals have privately incurred. We could discuss free enterprise, free sex, free basing, or any other liberty— all of which carry a massive price tag from their master. The question now is not *whether* we'll be in slavery but *to whom and under what conditions.*

"Slavery" can be defined as commitment. Many people dupe themselves into believing they don't have any commitments and don't answer to anyone. Theirs is the greater bondage. They quickly find themselves in meaningless jobs, welfare lines, miserable marriages, emergency rooms, cells, and finally, the morgue. These, too, are commitments. But remember that we *do* have a choice of masters and one of them offers a much lighter yoke. The Master I proclaim understands the needs of a slave firsthand.

Consider for a moment the society into which Jesus was born and in which He carried out His ministry of compassion. Here's what Nobel Prize winner Boris Pasternak said in his celebrated novel, *Dr. Zhivago.*[1]

> Rome was a flea market of borrowed gods and conquered peoples, a bargain basement on two floors, earth and heaven, a mass of filth convoluted in a triple knot as in an internal obstruction. Dacians, Herculians, Scythians, Samaritans, Hyperboreans, heavy wheels without spokes, eyes sunk in fat, sodomy, double chins, illiterate emperors, fish fed on the flesh of learned slaves . . . all crammed into the passages of the Coliseum, and all wretched.
>
> And then, into this tasteless heap of gold and marble He came, light and clothed in an aura, emphatically human, deliberately provincial, Galilean, and at that moment gods and nations ceased to be and man came into being—man the carpenter, man the plowman, man the shepherd with his flock of sheep at sunset, man who does not sound in the least proud, man thankfully celebrated in all the cradle songs of mothers and in all the picture galleries the world over.

COMMITMENT JESUS-STYLE

Jesus, who committed His life to the will of God the Father, demands the same from us.

He was known as a friend of publicans and

sinners. He certainly was not the well-combed, blue-eyed, filtered-down, reminted Jesus so widely portrayed in classical art. Jesus knew what He was doing, even if no one else did. He was well aware of the level of His commitment to the Father—a commitment that ultimately would take Him to a hill outside Jerusalem where He would be scandalized in public between two petty thieves. No romanticized shepherd with a delicate lamb on his shoulder. No "pale Galilean," this man. No, a thousand times no! He was commitment and miracle together.

The announcement of His birth was miraculous. His conception was divine. His life, words, deeds, and compassion were all set in the context of the impossible. His commitment to a lost world was so extreme that He never flinched at the thought of giving His life to give us a life that would never end.

Commitment—Jesus-style. To His disciples, He was often an enigma wrapped in mystery. Still, Jesus stayed with them, teaching, exhorting, scolding, loving. About little children, Jesus said, "Let them come to me, for this is what the kingdom of heaven is made of"—helpless little ones who compel adults to preserve them through commitment.

How did Jesus treat the prostitutes, tax collectors, and other unsightly people? Jesus rejected the narrow standards of the religious leadership of His day because He was more interested in completing His mission than obeying temple tradition. He'd come to heal those who needed a doctor—the sick of mind, body, and spirit, so He had no problem spending time with the riffraff. Because they *knew* they needed to recommit their lives, He loved them like they'd never been loved before. Lives were changed, priorities rearranged, commitments made to last forever.

Lives are still being changed every day. I'm an example; perhaps you are too. His commitment to us lives on, but where do our commitments lie? He has chosen us to bring light and hope to a needy world through our commitment to Him. "Commit your way to the Lord; trust in him, and he will act" (Ps. 37:5, RSV). "Commit your work to the Lord, and your plans will be established" (Prov. 16:3, RSV). "Chosen and destined by God the Father and sanctified by the Spirit for obedience to Jesus Christ and for sprinkling with his blood . . ." (1 Peter 1:2, RSV). God and Christ invite us to commit ourselves to become fellow slaves to their expanding family.

SUSPICIONS CONFIRMED

There's nothing easy about making or keeping commitments, especially when there always seems to be someone gleefully kicking the legs out from under your chair every time you lean back to think. In *The Screwtape Letters*, C.S. Lewis outlines an imaginary correspondence between the Devil, Screwtape, and his nephew Wormwood. Here Wormwood is on assignment to earth to bedevil a human.[2]

. . . the thing to avoid is the total commitment. Whatever he (the man) says, let his inner resolution be not to bear whatever comes to him, but to bear it "for a reasonable period"—and let the reasonable period be shorter than the trial is likely to last. It need not be much shorter; in attacks on patience, chastity and fortitude, the fun is to make the man yield just when (had he but known it) relief was almost in sight.

FEARDOM

From the apostle John, we learn that "fear hath torment" (1 John 4:18, KJV). Let's examine some torments to discover the keys that will help us escape them.

Afraid of failing? Welcome to the club. No one wants to fail, but we need to put failure into its proper perspective. Consider the track record of these famous failures.

Babe Ruth, long considered by the sports world to be the greatest athlete of all time, was famous for setting the home run record. Before Reggie Jackson, he failed so many times that he set the record for strike-outs.

Henry Ford failed and went broke five times before he succeeded in making his car and his name a household name.

Theodore Geisel was walking home with his manuscript in hand. He had just come from a meeting with a publisher, who had given him his twenty-third rejection notice. Near home, he bumped into an old college friend who happened to be an editor of children's books. Within minutes, Geisel signed a contract for his book, which is now in its twentieth printing. As one of the world's most successful authors of children's books, he is best known by his pen name—Dr. Seuss.

Winston Churchill did not become prime minister of England until he was sixty-seven. His greatest contribution to England came when he was a senior citizen.

Richard Hooker worked for seventeen years on a war story laced with inexhaustible humor. Predictably, it was torpedoed by no less than twenty-one publishers; nevertheless, he kept submitting it. Most of us have seen the movie or the television program based on Hooker's book—M*A*S*H.

Pretty impressive failures! You may say, "I'm not a writer, or a prime minister, or an inventor, or . . ." Perhaps not, but you'll never know what you *can* be until you say, "Whatever I choose to do, I will do well; I won't quit until I'm finished."

Successful people normally fail more times than a failure because failures quit after two or three disappointments. Winners can fail ten, fifty, or a thousand times before success, but they never stop at failure.

Perhaps, it's not fear of failure that worries you. Maybe, it's . . .

FEAR OF CRITICISM

People may say to you, "Look, you know we've never done it that way before," or "The top floor isn't going to like this idea," or "You want to go *where* on vacation? Europe? Now where are we going to get the money for that?"

It's tough to be criticized, especially if it's done with a hurtful or condescending attitude. Unless we are strong in our commitment to a person, an idea, or a cause, we may respond to criticism by simply giving up. It's been said the average person goes to a silent grave with a lifetime of wonderful melodies still unplayed. So many creative ideas are forever unexpressed for the fear of criticism.

FEAR OF HARD WORK

The greatest enemy within us is a dull, smug complacency. Easy Street ends in a blind alley. Life pays its dividends toward the end of the journey, not at the beginning. The real winners in life work hard for what they get. But what about the great people who've blessed us with their art, science, and invention? Did their genius come easily? Let's listen to some of them.

Thomas Edison said, "Genius is one percent inspiration, ninety-nine percent perspiration."

Michelangelo said, "If people knew how hard I worked to attain my mastery, it wouldn't seem so wonderful after all."

Carlyle, British man of letters, wrote, "Genius is the capacity for taking infinite pains."

Paderewski said, "A genius? Perhaps. But before I was a genius, I was a drudge."

Hard work? Yes. Great rewards? Absolutely! And they are there for us to receive. But first we have to break free from fears that keep us from achieving our potential. Free from *fear*dom requires commitment.

Everyday we make a choice. Either we drift downstream with the current where one master is waiting to watch us tumble over the waterfall of eternal death. Or we work our way upstream against the onrush of humanity for another master who offers the headwaters of eternal life. "No servant can serve two masters; for either he will hate the one and love the other, or he will be devoted to the one and despise the other. You cannot serve God and mammon" (Luke 16:13, RSV).

You cannot escape slavery. Both masters are calling for a commitment. Which one will you answer?

> The best reformers the world has ever seen are those who commence on themselves.
>
> G.B. Shaw

9

Your Place in History

As we have discovered, the need for commitment is great; the challenge, enormous. Now let's explore another reason for harnessing the power of commitment—a reason that stretches from earth to sky.

What would it be like to be *the* Rockefeller or *the* Ford or *the* president of the United States? Most people whose names hold instant recognition find themselves robbed of simple liberties. It would be wrong to couple our motivation to the empty train of recognition. After all, names like Manson, Eichmann, Hitler, and many others are world renowned, too.

Fame, fortune, and recognition can come our way as the result of persistent commitment. How sure and how grand this law of creation can be for us! According to Goethe, "He who is firm and resolute in will molds the world to himself."

One name fixed firmly in history is Colonel Andrew Rowan. His story was immortalized through a short article written by Elbert Hubbard in 1899. Much to the surprise of everyone, including Hubbard, this true story about commitment attracted phenomenal attention. By 1913, it had been translated into every written language, distributed to the opposing armies in the war between Russia and Japan, and reprinted in over two hundred magazines. Forty million copies were reported in print—the largest circulation of any literary venture ever attained during the lifetime of the author.

The hero of the story, the man who carried the message, was Colonel Andrew Summers Rowan, who, when the Spanish-American War broke out, was a young lieutenant in the U.S. Army. He was proposed for the difficult mission by the chief of the Bureau of Military Intelligence when President McKinley requested the name of a suitable envoy.

Lieutenant Rowan was sent at once, alone and unguarded. When he landed secretly on Cuba, he was furnished with native guides by Cuban patriots. His adventures, by his own modest account, were beset by obstacles, but he managed to make his way through the interior to deliver his message to General Garcia, who was in charge of the revolutionary forces.

There were certainly many fortuitous circumstances connected with the endeavor, but it was the sheer courage and indomitable spirit of the young lieutenant that were at the heart of his success. Rowan was decorated for his mission by the commander of the United States Army, who said, "I regard this achievement as one of the most hazardous and heroic deeds in military warfare." This was undoubtedly true, but for his character and level of commitment, rather than his military prowess, Lieutenant Andrew Summers Rowan will hold his place in history.

Here's an abbreviated version of that classic story *A Message to Garcia.*[1]

In all this Cuban business there is one man stands out on the horizon of my memory like Mars at Perihelion.

When war broke out between Spain and the United States, it was very necessary to communicate quickly with the leader of the Insurgents. Garcia was somewhere in the mountain vastnesses of Cuba—no one knew where. No mail or telegraph message could reach him. The President must secure his co-operation, and quickly.

What to do!

Someone said to the President, "There is a fellow by the name of Rowan who will find Garcia for you, if anybody can."

Rowan was sent for and given a letter to be delivered to Garcia. How the "fellow by the name of Rowan" took the letter, sealed it up in an oilskin pouch, strapped it over his heart, in four days landed by night off the coast of Cuba from an open boat, disappeared into the jungle, and in three weeks came out on the other side of the Island, having traversed a hostile country on foot and delivered his letter to Garcia—are things I have no special desire now to tell in detail. The point that I wish to make is this: McKinley gave Rowan a letter to be delivered to Garcia; Rowan took the letter and did not ask, "Where is he at?"

By the Eternal! There is a man whose form should be cast in deathless bronze and the statue placed in every college of the land. It is not book-learning young men need, nor instruction about this and that, but a stiffening of the vertebrae which will cause them to be loyal to a trust, to act promptly, concentrate their energies: to do the thing—"Carry a message to Garcia."

General Garcia is dead now, but there are other Garcias. No man who has endeavored to carry out an enterprise where many hands are needed, but has been well-nigh appalled at times by the imbecility of the average man—the inability or unwillingness to concentrate on a thing and do it. . . .

Slipshod assistance, foolish inattention, dowdy indifference, and half-hearted work seem the rule; and no man succeeds, unless by hook or crook or threat he forces or bribes other men to assist him; or mayhap, God in His goodness performs a miracle, and sends him an Angel of Light for an assistant.

My heart goes out to the man who does his work

when the "boss" is away, as well as when he is at home. And the man who, when given a letter for Garcia, quietly takes the missive, without asking any idiotic questions, and with no lurking intention of chucking it into the nearest sewer, or of doing aught else but deliver it, never gets "laid off," nor has to go on a strike for higher wages. Civilization is one long, anxious search for just such individuals. Anything such a man asks shall be granted. He is wanted in every city, town and village—in every office, shop, store and factory. The world cries out for such; he is needed and needed badly—the man who can *carry a message to Garcia.*

For being a faithful messenger, Colonel Rowan has earned a name in the literary heavens like the planet Mars at Perihelion—the brightest place in its orbit around the sun. For service as a faithful messenger, we can earn even greater brilliance. Understanding this great opportunity starts with an understanding of some of the simpler truths. We're probably all familiar with "Desiderata," the free-form observation about life and its choices. Because of its universal appeal, posters and plaques quoting "Desiderata" have been distributed all over the world. One section is particularly inspiring to me.[2]

DESIDERATA—THE DESIRABLES

You are a child of the universe,
no less than the trees and the stars;

you have a right to be here.
And whether or not it is clear to you,
no doubt the universe is unfolding as it should.

How is the "universe unfolding as it should" and where is our place of preeminence in history? The prophet Daniel was given a vision even too profound for him to understand. "Go thy way, Daniel: for the words are closed up and sealed until the time of the end . . . but the wise shall understand" (Dan.12:9, 10, KJV).

Today, because so much of God's plan for the universe has "unfolded" through Christ, we can understand. Examine the prophecy's promise. "And they that be wise shall shine as the brightness of the firmament; and they that turn many to righteousness as the stars for ever and ever" (Dan. 12:3, 4, KJV). That's how it's possible for us to have a place in history even greater than Mars at its brightest.

The prophet reminds us of the qualifications for this celestial place, "At that time thy people shall be delivered, every one that shall be found written in the book" (Dan. 12:1, KJV). Just as Colonel Andrews's name was written in Hubbard's book for an act that took place primarily in secret, so we too can be confident about private acts of spiritual commitment being written in God's book.

How much more fulfilling can our lives become if we actually believe that He who records the intents of the heart has the ability and the desire to give us a place in history that outshines the stars? No matter how you answer that question, a commitment to commitment can place your name in history.

> Ideas won't keep: something
> must be done about them.
>
> A. N. Whitehead

10

A Commitment Checklist

His mother thought he should become a teacher; his dad wanted him to sing. This dilemma hounded Luciano Pavarotti as he grew up in Modena, Italy. Desiring to please both his parents, he pursued both fields—singing lessons and teachers' college. Upon graduation, the frustration became too much. "Shall I be a teacher or a singer?" he asked his father. "Luciano," said his father, "if you try to sit on two chairs, you will fall between them. For life, you must choose one chair."

We know what choice Pavarotti made. After seven years of sweat, toil, and study, he made his first professional appearance; after seven more years, the Metropolitan Opera. Later, he observed, "Whether it's laying bricks, driving a straight nail, writing a book, whatever we choose we should give ourselves to it. Commitment, that's the key."[1]

We've seen many "chairs" in these chapters and how people have chosen theirs. Now let's step back for a moment and summarize the keys we've discovered to seek our own personal fulfillment. As Robert Schuller says, "Commitment is at the top of my list of seven life-changing human values. Commitment is where living really begins." Then, let's live!

THREE STEPS TOWARD MAKING A COMMITMENT

1. Make a decision.
2. Act upon your decision.
3. Continue to act.

Do not be discouraged. Commitment conquers. Examine this encouraging story from *Success Unlimited*.[2]

> In a gun factory in the United States, an unusual experiment was conducted. A bottle cork, weighing less than four grams, was suspended by an almost invisible silk thread alongside a heavy steel bar, itself hung vertically from a beam by a slender metal chain.
>
> The cork, set in motion, began to swing gently against the steel bar. For a long time, there was nothing to be seen but its rhythmic, noiseless sway-

ing back and forth, while the bar remained motionless.

More minutes went by—two, five, ten, a half hour. Then suddenly under the relentless barrage, and so nearly imperceptibly as to seem almost an illusion, the steel bar was seen to tremble. A few moments later, it shuddered as if seized with a nervous tremor, hung quiet again, then shuddered again.

There was no deviation in the motion of the cork. Steadily, without haste, it continued its noiseless assaults. And now the movements of the great steel bar became less tremulous as it settled into the beginning of an orderly pattern of motion, gradually picking up the rhythm of the swinging cork.

In another half-hour, the cork, its work finished, had been cut down and the heavy bar was swinging back and forth as steadily and as rhythmically as a pendulum.

How many steel bars have imprisoned you and your ambition? Maybe, you should crash through them with the persistent cork of commitment.

The clues we uncovered along the road of commitment bring to mind another useful analogy.

WHY COMMITMENT IS LIKE RIDING
A BICYCLE

1. You must *believe* that a contraption that can't even stand up by itself will transport you safely.
2. You must let go of all other forms of

support and balance yourself with the
sheer force of momentum.
3. You have to lean into the curves.
4. You can coast for a while, but you won't get
far if you don't keep pedaling.

To whom are we committed? Everyone assumed
Bela Karolyi was committed to Romania when he
coached Nadia Comaneci to Olympic gold in 1976.
But one year after the 1980 Olympics, he defected
to the United States for more freedom to pursue
his true commitment—women's gymnastics.
Mary Lou Retton, all-around women's gymnastic
gold medalist in 1984, was his first accomplish-
ment in the United States. Lest anyone judge
Karolyi too harshly for defecting to remain with
his first love, beware of those who defect *from*
their first love. How about the family who assumes
Dad is committed to Mom and the kids until he
walks out? How about the customer who assumes
the sales-clerk is committed to the product and
the store until he sells for the competition?

Here's a sobering, but understandable statistic
reported in 1984. Ninety percent of those who
volunteer to become missionaries never go.[3] How
do you respond to such reality? How should we
respond? "I appeal to you therefore, brethren, by
the mercies of God, to present your bodies as a
living sacrifice, holy and acceptable to God, which
is your spiritual worship" (Rom. 12:1, RSV).

SEVEN PRACTICAL STEPS TO HELP
CHANGE *YOUR* WORLD

1. Make a personal commitment to change the world.
2. Ask God to help you gain greater sensitivity to the needs of those around you.
3. Search the Scriptures to discover how God Himself sees the world.
4. Remember that the world includes your neighbor or spouse, as well as people in other countries.
5. Ask God to guide you how to work to change the world.
6. Take one step at a time. Act upon what you now know, as you ask God to show you more.
7. Be patient and steadfast.

"Go therefore and make disciples of all nations, baptizing them in the name of the Father and of the Son and of the Holy Spirit, teaching them to observe all that I have commanded you; and lo, I am with you always, to the close of the age" (Matt. 28:19, 20, RSV). Changing the world requires commitment. Let's review what commitment means for us.

COMMITMENT IS . . .

Not trying, but doing.
Seeking the opposite of *omit*ment.

Changing maybe into certainly.
Putting others first without a second thought.
Sharing good news after it's old to you.
Doing things that please an absent friend.
Like being pregnant: You either are or you aren't.
Leaving your warm bed when a small voice says,
  "I'm cold."
Spending two years teaching a child how to walk
  and talk and eighteen years explaining how
  to sit down and be quiet.
Enjoying a visit, before you've gone and after you
  return.
Learning to love the things you hate to do.
Burning your bridges behind you, not in front of
  you.
Aiming at a target that most people cannot even
  see and hitting it.
Life sharing.
Reading inspirational books through to the last
  chapter.

Remember, as Robert Schuller says, "Great people are ordinary people with extraordinary amounts of determination."

These pages have been a wide-ranging, galloping journey. Doubtless we could still fill hundreds of pages with inspirational examples of commitment. J.C. Penney and his sacrifice to the inner-city poor; Oregon Senator Mark Hatfield and his courageous voice of conscience in opposition to Vietnam; Peter Ueberroth's debt-free Olympics in Los Angeles, and the list is endless.

I conclude with one of the most powerful elements of true commitment—prayer. "How do I know what I think until I see what I say?"[4] This apt quote applies to interpersonal communication and, I think, even more to our communication with God. How do I know what I want and need until I see what I ask? I don't know about you, but many times, the answers I get from God tell me that I might have been praying the wrong prayer.

I prayed for food, God gave me a tool.

I prayed for shelter, God cleared the skies.

I prayed for clothing, God gave me the shirt off another's back.

I prayed for a car, God delivered a bus schedule.

I prayed for a wife, God introduced me to the bride of Christ.

I prayed for money, God sent His servants to help.

I prayed for strength, God taught me the power of weakness.

I prayed for faith, God introduced me to patience.

I prayed for others, God showered me with blessings and sent me to serve.

While writing this book, I prayed that God would open my eyes to the larger vision of commitment. One of the first things He did was close my eyes with tears—tears of joy over the accomplishments of those who had every reason to cry, but chose instead to *do something.* If, while reading this book, you have shared those tears with me, then you and I and all who are written in this book belong to the same family.

The week of June 20, 1983, Pioneer 10 crossed out of our solar system, 2.8 billion miles away. As the first man-made object to escape the sun's gravity, it bears a message from its maker. Using pictures of a man, a woman, the sun, planet earth, and the scientific language of numbers, it spells out our name, defines our common anatomy, and points to our home. Thus, a lone relic races through the universe to proclaim a simple message: My creators are one family. Its message is clear to anyone who might recover and decode this galactic greeting card. How clear is its message to you?

Trained by the Father to serve this worldwide family, you hold the key to your personal fulfillment now and forever. Here's your overriding commitment. Let me close using Lee Iacocca's words, with one small change of massive proportions, " my Father and I will be forever grateful."

Notes

Chapter 1

[1] Hal Butler, *Sports Heroes Who Wouldn't Quit* (New York: Simon & Schuster, Inc., 1973), 46.

[2] Ibid., pp. 52, 53.

[3] Geoffrey C. Ward, *Success Magazine* (April 1985): 55, 56.

[4] *Encyclopaedia Britannica*, 15th ed., Vol. 28 (Chicago: Encyclopedia Britannica, Inc., 1985), 36.

Chapter 2

[1] Art Linkletter (Chicago: Nightingale-Conant Corp., 1983). Single cassette recording.

[2] Ibid.

[3] Lee Iacocca, *Iacocca: An Autobiography* (New York: Bantam Books, Inc.), xv.

Chapter 3

[1] Nido Qubein, *Get the Best from Yourself* (New Jersey: Prentice-Hall, Inc., 1983), 38.

[2] Butler, *Sports Heroes Who Refused to Quit,* 117-125.

[3] Guy Burke, *Cornerstones of Communication* (Altadena: Burke Communication Services, 1984), 2.

[4] From *Christopher News Notes,* No. 259.

Chapter 4

[1] C. S. Lewis, *The Great Divorce* (New York: Macmillan, Inc., 1970), 18.

[2] David A. Wiessler, *U.S. News & World Report* (Oct. 3, 1983): 66.

[3] Staff writer, *Time* (Oct. 29, 1979): 87.

[4] Staff writer, *U.S. News & World Report* (Oct. 3, 1983): 66.

[5] *Los Angeles Times,* 16 June 1985, pt. I.

Chapter 5

[1] Staff writer, *U.S. News & World Report* (Oct. 3, 1983): 66.

[2] Herbert V. Prochnow and Herbert V. Prochnow, Jr., *The Public Speaker's Treasure Chest* (New York: Harper & Row, 1964), 286.

Chapter 6

[1] *Grolier Encyclopedia,* Vol. 2 (New York: Grolier Society, Inc., 1950), 376.

[2] Selected by Hazel Felleman, *Best Loved Poems of the American People* (Garden City, New York: Doubleday & Co., 1936), 38.

[3] Roger Golde, *What You Say Is What You Get* (New York: Hawthorn Books, Inc. 1979), chap. 3.

[4] Iacocca, *Iacocca: An Autobiography,* 4, 340.

Chapter 7

[1] *Los Angeles Times,* 16 June 1985, pt. I.

[2] Art Williams, "A Quality Called Commitment," *Saturday Evening Post*(Dec. 1983): 97.

Chapter 8

[1] Boris Pasternak, quoted in *Dr. Zhivago* (New York: Pantheon Books Inc. 1958), 43.

2 C. S. Lewis, *The Screwtape Letters* (New York: Macmillan Publishing Co., 1951), 142.

Chapter 9

1 Elbert Hubbard, *Message to Garcia* (Mt. Vernon, N.Y.: Peter Pauper Press, 1977), 17.

2 Max Ehrmann, *Poems of Max Ehrmann*, edited by Bertha Ehrmann (Boston: Bruce Humphries, Inc., 1948), 83.

Chapter 10

1 Luciano Pavarotti, "Choose One Chair," *Guideposts* (March 1985): 40.

2 Marjorie Spiller Neagle, "Success Unlimited," *A Treasury of Success Unlimited*, Edited by Og Mandino (New York: Simon & Schuster, 1966), 81.

3 Jim Elliot, *Global Prayer Digest* (Frontier Fellowship, Inc., May 1984), Day 21.

4 Roger Golde, *What You Say Is What You Get*, 10.